One Last Cigarette
By Mary Stone Dockery
Honest Publishing

All Rights Reserved
© 2013 Mary Stone Dockery
ISBN 978-09571427-4-9

Manufactured in the United Kingdom
by Lightning Source UK Limited

One Last Cigarette

Mary Stone Dockery

I

I Can Leave You Like I Leave	9
Evening Litany	10
Heat Wave	11
When the Bourbon Settles	13
Researchers Discover Insomniac Birds are the Sexiest Birds*	14
Still Life with Tea and Book	15
Portrait of a Couple with an Overdrawn Checking Account	16
Here, We Like the Cupboards Cobwebbed	17
Woman Discovers Creepy Ex-Boyfriend Living in Attic*	18
Before the Diagnosis	19
Red Wine Apologies	20
Bury	22
Winter Myths	23
August Ghosts	24
Settling In	26

II

Pisces Elegy	31
Overflow	33
Arsonist	35
He Drew Me From Behind	37
Where to Place Hands	39
A Night without Stars	40
The First Time	42
Rising Action	43
Alone, Before His Birth	44
Long Summer	45
My Mother's Ghost Returns	47
Because Another Person Asked When We'd Start Having Children	48

Self-Portrait with Aftermath	49
Thursday Autobiography: Astronomers Reveal Supernova Factory	50
After Hours	51
Belated	52
Restless Wonder	53

III

June's Child	59
Morning Comes	60
Why I Can't Return Your Call	61
Becoming Windows	62
Remains	64
We Stop Writing About the Moon	65
What We Have Forgotten	67
Autopsy of Me	68
After Moving	69
Poem for Fire	71
The Emptiness Begins	73
The Widower	74
Sister	75
Preface to a Late Night Text	77
At Dawn	78
Bone Cartography	79

IV

Quit Day	83
Love Letter for Virtual Particles	85
The Widow	86
What a Lover Asks	88
On Our Last Visit	89
Uptight Flamingos Will Only Have Sex to Marvin Gaye Slow Jams*	90
Portrait of a Girl Drawn with Neophobia	92
The Meaning of More	93
Your Name is a Shape Made in the Mouths of Magicians	94
Poem for Apology	95
Reaches And	96
Our Home Becomes an Island	98
Final Quiet	99
The Ways We Wake	101
Digging for Wasps	102

* *Title taken from a Jezebel.com article*

I

I Can Leave You Like I Leave

whispers dangling at doorframes,
morning, formaldehyde fingers
and reflections of a ghost in some earring
left alone on a table, the taste of a chalky scar
splitting a lover's abdomen

You dress like *father* when there is no father
or when father becomes mother becomes son becomes sky

I've yet to find where you've hoarded the cigarettes

I have held you in my hands like a glass globe
imagined the burning flakes within

I allowed you inside me
a gloomy fog seeking each crack   the last comfort
burden clinging to a winter coat.

this confusion of bitter
teeth hitting the glass rim

mother brings envelopes filled with your name
father burns them, believes the smoke
will draw us together   believes
you will exhale my love and take it with you
wrapped tight in a blue baby blanket

A lighter in your pocket bangs in the dryer
our basement a tomb of lonely brick
collector of sound

Evening Litany

Night waters remain unmoved. The calm is lightning. We wait to be placed within the substance of night. Our bodies, our tumors. Night arrives as cancered graffiti, all etching and cobalt handwritten. We step through black halos. Wait again for the inevitable necrosis of the sky. If we have altered the cells around us, we know it's called progression, and our tissue expanding beneath a microscope is like a video of a supernova or an ocean. Blood will always remind us of flying. The light of the moon resembles a tidal wave upon your face. The ground beneath us vibrates. Nothing else moves. It's as if we are swallowed in a dream-sea of our own making. Others have calm seas, perhaps calm dreams. There is brutality in the night spilling open. You say, *metastasizing*. I say, *want*.

Heat Wave

Yesterday, I was done with cigarettes,
caught my lungs in the laundry basket
dangling there like lace panties.

The man came to the door
asking to fill milk jugs
with smoke I curled into my fists.

I began but couldn't finish,
wanted the scent braided
into my skin, to hold myself

beneath a microscope, slice a cell
open, breathe into it, feel my body
contract or stand against the blinking

windows, find the rain, the hurricanes.
There are many ways to experience
breathing, to find yourself

deep in scents that forgive you
for only a moment, then thrust
you back against a wall.

I am mostly incompetent
in remembering, keep the laundry
outside for too long, let the smoke

alarm bleed the walls.
Sometimes clean sheets drape
my rooms and I see ghosts

outside, bitter smoke
rising from the gutters.

When the Bourbon Settles

We dream vintage   sunsets,
long hungers, the drone of car rides.
Highways, steam. When it snows, I
call too early, a steamboat on my lips.
What words have we lost   to those
old postcard highways? Think of the
scatter, what we dropped behind us
as easily   as   cigarette butts.
Smoke the color of your mother's
wedding dress. In what hour did we
pluck the first plum as a silent prayer?
When you look at me I am finished
with the smoke-stacks, the stockyards,
the steel. It was always something else
we wanted, draped over   another
couple's shoulder,   a scent we never
noticed, lonely mist,   cough of a
falling tree, the simple idea of drifting.

Researchers Discover Insomniac Birds are the Sexiest Birds

We've been awake since May
and already, August threads
its feathers into us, asking
to see just one shut eye.
We find melatonin pills
sprinkled in the hallway,
crushed on the kitchen counter
next to suspicious straws
and smelling of our mouths.
Of course we ignore any call
for sleep - our bodies accustomed
to moon milk and dimly lit back porches.
In the shower, your back spreads
over my feet a sexy shadow-wing
or I am hallucinating again
and keep finding you
on television screens, written
into crumbled grocery lists,
hiding in the wallpaper.
And night never comes.
We've forgotten what it tastes like
in the dark with beer
fumbling for a flashlight
and we make love sometimes
on the carpet just to know
clouds of the floor.
The bed is a hologram,
a memory of some other
dreamy couple.

Still Life with Tea and Book

Add arms. Take them away. Add a vase, then two roses. Draw them without buds. Just stems and leaves. Add thorns. Put a crack in the vase. Add more thorns. The tablecloth should checker in black and white, fade off in corners. Threads poke out, blackened. A hole on one corner where you rubbed too long with a wet rag. Coffee stains like pieces of escaped silhouette. Don't spill the sugar bowl. Leave a spoon on the table dry, a bowl filled with dusk. Draw my shadow into the picture, my edges burned, blurred. You have always drawn me with smeared borders. Why stop now? Go further. Obscure our desire into the wrinkles of a flower stem, this green pointing finger. Conceal silk and rum between the lines. A confusion of petals or bangs. Make me mist, then distort our touching with razor-blue lips.

Portrait of a Couple with an Overdrawn Checking Account

One more rainless day, a corn husk
    flutters into the lawn, cracks beneath
your boots. We've enjoyed these
    sidewalks as if they were long arms
carrying us from one place to another,
    and even though we never travel far
we know it's necessary movement.
    I've finished packing bags of give-away
clothes, wait in the front room
    with a cigarette and the yearning
for something else to burn the tongue.
    Without money, we've learned
how to find faces in shapes on the tile,
    in the patterns on the bathroom wall.
How to make macaroni and cheese
    a main course dish, how to gamble
our last few quarters on claw machines.
    How to nap just to rid ourselves
of another day. How to put something off
    for days, like the old coats in the closet
or too many unused containers of coriander.
    How to re-use words like *sorry*
and *can't*. How to want.

Here, We Like the Cupboards Cobwebbed

Robins without wings, grounded, headstones
engraved in the backyard stacked
and ready: Try moving from one side
of the room to the next without looking
out the window. Watch your lover
disappear. If only to see the room whole.
When you walk against the light,
you produce seventeen shadows
that all need named, each one shaped
like a bee's mouth. You look for jaws
on doorknobs. Other words for *fly*.
The windows here only remember
first names: *Dear home, how come
your sail slackens in the light?*
We have tried to prove the haunted house
theory through electrical currents
and recordings, listened for names
murmured within white noise,
though we have eaten our fill
of radiation, and have been warmed.
Lovers have many names
and appear only in mirrors.
Light bulbs and shiny objects
concern us now, as they reflect
the hysteria of a home
draped in mosquito wings,
mouths full of beetles.

Woman Discovers Creepy Ex-Boyfriend Living in Her Attic

Night reminds me of your beer breath. What color
the world is after a night rain. Three years after
our break-up, I still find half-full Blue Moon bottles.
Our relationship aged while I smoked cigarettes,
curled my hair, dreamt of more. Before you left,
my hair grew so long you could braid it to the bedposts.
We spent too many mornings laughing off nausea,
spilling all the honey. Sometimes I still crave
the cold touch of porcelain, mornings with your hands
on the back of my neck, the orchestra of some
old film playing over our kitchen fights.
You taught me that orgasms equal love,
that night is night for as long as the sun can stain
our curtains yellow, for as long as we allow
ourselves to fade into walls. When friends visit,
I talk of the handsome ghost playing with my hair
before I go to sleep, dream of your body
dangling from a dark ceiling, waiting to touch.
When you watch me touch myself, hear me call out
your name and the names of our lovers,
it's as if we are back in the same room
and the beer is cold again, smoke sculpting
our faces into the sheets.

Before the Diagnosis

A bird staggers in the bathroom, flapping against the mirror like you've done so many times.

We wake to feathers, the tile draped with galaxies. We drop them out the window, watch them land on concrete without disintegrating.

A lure of bones and beaks. Later, when I see robins next to headstones, I will find you watching me.

Patterns exist in memories. The moon wipes them with olive oil. Smears them across the ground.

Only days before, I find you molting on our bedroom floor, the sound like ripping silk. How do you say earthquake after shedding the love letters?

You look in the mirror one last time, pull barbs and quills from your cheeks.

Behind you, I adjust your beak. Your crying like crows stumbling over lakes.

An empty bird cage on the window sill. Later, I'll discover your nail clippings and an empty bottle of whiskey standing upright, waiting to be moved.

Red Wine Apologies

On the motorcycle,
the wind cut up our thighs.
Left us raw, red.
I clung to the back of your shirt
a flag drifting then snapping
against you.

The next day, your chapped lips cracked
against my cheek.

*

I told one lie, and then another.
There is a space between those words
needing corked.

*

The spots on our wine glasses
remain after several washings.

You run your finger over the glass rim.
The whine, your song, makes me numb.

*

A good wine enters the room.
A good wine is bodied, generous,
spills on your slacks,
sneaks into the cracks of a table
and smells in the morning – violet,

vanilla, a hint of fried egg.
A good wine finishes itself.
A good wine tastes like the letter "r"
and its different colors
in other languages,
signals to its lover
when it is time to go,
listens, then clings
to the tongue.
A good wine tastes like pearl.
A good wine bites its lip
when it feels sexiest,
opens berry into the air above it
and settles in the mouth, soft.
A good wine loses lovers.
A good wine looks good
in white all year long.

*

At dinner, the knife scrapes
the plate. Your steak, rare
bleeds onto the potatoes.
Your foot touches mine
and I shift away from you.
We speak into our wine glasses,
hold silence in our mouths
like hot grapes.

Bury

I keep meeting you
where trains forget their whistles
the wind bony

we lack frames, our skeletons
collaged rust and iron

At the bridge
we bury an old memory
in your flask

the remains scattered
along tracks below
so many diary pages, burned

Our favorite memories
reside within that fire

scorched shadows
that siren up the mountain-side

We consider
the surprise of wild fires

lift the pages
gently, what stories
we find in papery jawbones

Winter Myths

We made love against mirrors.

We captured cicadas to add to boring recipes.

You broke a silver spoon across my back. My vertebrae shifted, each one growing its own wing. You plucked the feathers one at a time and ate them, the taste of sky. Whiskey-drenched intimacy.

We re-named ourselves after guitars. Strummed tree bark with numb fingers. Beneath rotted trees.

Decaying barns fell around us. Splinter. We took pictures of barn bodies. Pasted them to our walls.

Maps of your hands flickered. Black lights. Cigarettes. Kissing in the dark. We bought moonstones by the hundreds. Fed them to our mothers and our fathers.

We built Decembers in the basement, furnace dolls and fever blooms. Each November smoldered against our hands. Ash-heavy. Leaf-ridden. We sold what we could on the street, colonies of cigarette burns braided into our hair. We made potpourri out of the leftovers. *June June.*

We destroyed dresses, hem-lined with pearl iridescence, anything with the scent of fingernail polish. We dabbed our palms in gasoline. Waited for bone wreckage. Its long silences. A sparrow flying through an empty living room.

August Ghosts

I'll say *One last cigarette*
and nearly mean it.
The road will turn gray and flat
the hills curling back behind us
our ex-lovers' murmurs
retreating to the river.
It is the river we wish
to turn from, the river
we hope to silence,
our lovers' faces sliced
by fins, silver flashes,
then nothing. There is no
sudden dark – only
what we unwrite across
one another's backs.
Each name a pebble
swollen and wet.
It is the river
you'll ask me
to flick the butt into,
the river we work to destroy.
In bed we swim backward
away from August ghosts,
what we promised so many others
the wild and the peonies
and the oak limbs scattering
across the river, so many teeth.

*

In the quiet, I read what ache
writes across your lips.
A river is only a river, you say,
and my hands, bloated in the heat
press July further into bone:
what geraniums smell like in death
your dry smile, this lonely room.
Each vine cut from a trellis
left reaching. For my lover,
I crawl beneath the porch
and gather sticks, which we
practice rubbing together
to find our voices, all we can do
with these summer months.
A river is more than a river, I say,
at night, with the moon
and our hands and our songs.
The way it levels itself
for traveling fish
and still makes no sound.

Settling In

A newly silent home
    locked doors, pulled curtains,
a lamp, its light-crusted shade,
    a dimness that reveals itself
only in sudden solitude.
    Afterthoughts of what follows
a great change – even in fantasy,
    trees need rain, the home
needs painted, the body
    needs a place to lie down.
Shadows in the living room or
    dark marrow waters uncurling
over the floor toward me
    where I sit with a new book
on an old chair, in an unexpected
    house, and listen for the amber stillness,
a silence filled with sounds
    we only hear when we're looking.
Where there was once certainty
    coiled at my feet like a sleeping cat,
remains a lack I'm unable to name.
    Alone, I'm sure the shadows
make the sound of a brush
    pulling through long, wet hair.

II

Pisces Elegy

It's as if the drums have always
been there on lonely sidewalks,
    each step a vibration, a tremble.
The drums follow me into the bedroom,

    where you examine a room in seizure: sheets
shiver, the walls throb. In the morning,
    you tell me how the rhythm keeps changing –
are we inside each other now? Can you hear

    steel breaking under water? Thumps,
bangs, currents in your pitched voice.
    Listen for the sound of brass bursting
against docks, and I follow it, find

your scaled skin lying crumpled in the grass,
    streaks that pulse and change beneath sunlight,
black flashes, red veins, herring bands and lines.
    Rays spill across, leading me to waves where

    the water swells, taunting me with a Pisces
surf, pretending it has never seen you.
    You ask me to surface from the black
cave I sit in, limbs dry as matchsticks,

you call, a swimming drum, and
    splashes of doubt push into us.
But I know better – I know water zips
    open and swallows. At night, the drums

arise in encore, and from beneath, muddled
    sounds are your vocal chords, angled again,
finned words, hooks, corruptions finally
    rippling the edges of black sands. You eat

other fish, swim alone, push against
    the sea's wet breath. It's what you have always
wanted. Your fins scrape the water
    as if you claw long, wet walls.

When we find one another in the same bed,
    our feet are no longer finned apart,
but propellers beneath gushing silk,
    and we sprain and curve into each other

arcs of hydration. Our lips part
    engaging the waters before us,
and the drumming bourgeons.

Overflow

You tell her you are done with this farm,
with the old tractors rusting in the timber,
the flood lines etched on the tin shed.
You remember how each flood
crept to the steps of the porch
as the levee tore –
the floating picnic table,
tying the boat to the flag pole.

The way houses become islands
is routine for you.

You can no longer count
the number of buoys anchored
near your garage door.

She speaks of the lives of trees,
braced in their early years
with tarnished rods, how slowly
they seem to grow, how suddenly
they shade what was once
open space.

When you look at her hands,
you think of water receding,
all the cracked mud.
These acres are concrete slabs,
the river but bristles on a broom,
sweeping away all the seeds.

When you look at her hands,
you think of piles of things after,
in buckets and truck beds,
the way everyone stopped to look.

Arsonist

After setting the fire, she left
wet matches on the dresser
and closed all the windows,

the doors, a scent of burned
paper and smoke tearing
up her thighs. She watched

from the road as the house burned –
in the window fire curled
into red pirouettes, its arms

twisting to the ceiling in ringlets,
its fingers orange-red and moving.

Hot gauze wrapped the wood, the walls,
waving at her, hissing her name.

She watched the building crinkle
with heat, blackening, raw,
heaving, felt its sparking nails

along her arms with each flick
against the wooden frame,
as if it were her skin; this house ached -

it would give in. She knelt
on the asphalt, rocks sticking in her knees

sharp knots in her throat hot iron. The warmth,
the way her house frowned before her
like a dream you can't recall
its edges scorched and burning.

She swayed beneath a lock
of smoke, trailing a thick
charcoal scent.

When the firemen arrived,
they stood in the street
where they waited,

pumping water into her
home. They vowed not to leave
till they finished, the sun
clawing their faces.

He Drew Me From Behind

He drew me from behind,
noting as his hand soothed the canvas,
how slender my neck appeared beneath
the bob of my hair.

I stood with one arm to my side,
feeling the warmth of the lights
on my naked backside.
I imagined his pencil outlining

the curve of my back,
the creases of my shoulder blades.
I was certain that in black and white
I would appear slender from neck to thigh,

as this is how he viewed me,
how his hands discovered me in the light.
I lodged my forearm over my eyes,
tempted to turn and touch his face,

but knew he smirked or frowned
depending on the location of his hand.
I could almost taste the lead,
him penciling in my shoulder.

I could almost feel his sweat as it dripped
onto my spine, the slide for his nerves.
He did not tell me to stop shaking
and I knew it was because neither of us could,

so I waited while he drew,
imagining the faceless back that only he had ever really seen,
remembering that this was the way he loved me,
back facing him, lying on my side
so as to not have to draw
the fear in my eyes.

Where to Place Hands

I take the scissors, cut strips from shirts, paper, robes. I will build a nest. The floor is like a game board or a boat deck. Here, we slip together. Catch flying bones and put them in our mouths. I will not destroy lust with these hands, with a complicated knot. We walk in and out of doorways. See the lines on the floor. Your heels all cut up. Remind me again what we search for. What we won't find. What color my hair used to be before you asked me to change it. How long ago we met. I've forgotten where to place my name. Your shoulder blade or the back porch. There are more bones in the kitchen, waiting to be nailed down. The casket scent follows you from the other room. Ghosts wave in all the doorways.

*

The smell of burning hair. Sweet. Charred honey. Each morning she twisted newspapers into violent bouquets and lit them on fire. Her hair got shorter. Began to fall out. She bought wigs at a store down the street and wore them to parties. She wore each one only once, then burned them in her bathtub. When neighbors began to complain, she bought exotic birds to cover the sound of fire, naming them after brothers and sisters and lovers. One night, her neighbors lined up outside her door, smoke the color of birds leaking beneath the door. Inside, ash. Inside, clouds disguised the moon. They found her later at a bar, a cold drink in her hand. A crow drawn on her bald head, she told the crowd what the feathers asked.

A Night Without Stars

It's not like I'd imagined, meeting you
here beside the aching tree.
I've wanted to climb this tree for years,
but it's branches have finally died
and we find them lying on the ground
like the scoured bones of a whale.

The clouds are not new, have been here
hovering since the other morning.
My mother called it a hemorrhaging sky
saying the weather man turned off
his machines and decided to let it come –
the thunder, snow, rain, the curling clouds
he'd kept hidden from his audience
for years. Later, the weather man
shot himself in his office after discovering
a cold front in his own living room
and mountains eroding beneath silk rivers,
the migration of black birds to his bedroom
carrying charred nests, feathered promises.

We talk about the weather man
while looking at the gray sky –
there is something mistaken about the color,
the way it's forgotten to darken with dusk.
As if the sun still reflects along some horizon
not far from here. Yet, we can't find
the light either, there are no stars, and
instead, too many moons here in the palms
of your hands and then your eyes. I can feel
each moon blink and pulse along my skin.

Beneath this shade of sky, our limbs
blend in with the branches of the dying tree.
We scour the soil hoping to dye it
with the shine of our breath.

We wonder what the white walls in that office
must have looked like after he pulled
the trigger. We consider the flash
during that same moment, how it
stained so many skies.

The First Time

The first lightning bolt, made of copper, drops against the home. Nails become static. The home shivers, lights up. Fire shapes across doors. You think you can catch the aftermath, these droplets from the sky shining metal stars, mouths opening. You are lost on porches for years in this imagining. What colors appear on your shelves, perched like birds? Instead of motion, there is only precision – a brush in your hand, a paint-by-number in the closet, a dead cockroach stuck at the top of a doorframe. Again, you remember. The sky's limiting scope. Barbed wire tangled across living room floors.

Rising Action

The winter that we found the bones. Epigraphs etched on a basement wall, fingers soft as already-white dandelions. Scatter, poof; nameless wonders. That season, of them all, was marked by cloud shadows, barbed wire, a lack of umbrellas. I stayed in, mostly. Only left the house to chip ice from a tree, only when we had whiskey. My mother spent her mornings looking out the window, painting the streetlamp across the street. We kept running out of yellow so she taught us how to bring the dark along, to lift it tenderly into small pouches or coffee cans. To hoard it for our silences. I was angry in ways I'd been warned. Despised my own name and saying it out loud. I was in love with the boys who seemed to move like cars, so many tires spinning. Every night meant fevers and listening. My breath sewed itself to the trees.

Alone, Before his Birth

It comes down to a memory: the candle aisle
in a Dollar General, bright tile, he moves
inside me, flipping, like a swollen kidney
shifting. A couple at the end of the aisle saying
Please don't do this here and I know it's tonight
but don't know yet what that means or how
to say it. I wave them away with one hand,
cradle what must be his head now
with my other, my fingernails searching
through a sweater. I feel the roundness
of him, the points and edges of what will later
reveal a small body, but now only feels
like a large rock, his body
wanting to be read by my hands, familiar
and unknown all at once, the lines
of his body brail for my panic. I wait
for the water, the fear, grip
him while he pushes down, how tight
I press him back toward my spine,
holding him in.

Long Summer

It was a good day
for porch sitting.
For eating cashews.
For dragging flowerbeds,
replacing day lilies
with pumpkin seeds.
For waiting.

She waited in her dark
where the mossy sunsets
forgot how long it had been.
A promise is a promise
is a promise.
Beyond the yard women
seemed to smile. The elegance
of her own hands
long bitten off.
What cracks she found
among her shadow.

There is a time
and a place for shame.
She had held it
in her hands before.
It burns.

In better times, she might have
remembered to check her watch.
To paint the patio table bronze
and place it in the sun.

She stayed where she could reach
her shadow. Feel it grieving
against her back like a loyal cat.

My Mother's Ghost Returns

Her rain-laced hand touches
a picket fence. White paint
fragments drop to the grass.
Home again. What remains
of a rusted swing set trembles
against the wind, a child's
backpack on the porch,
where the evening left it.
The table has been cleared
in the kitchen, except
for a bowl of cereal
and pink milk.
She steps on crayons
scattered in the hallway,
and they snap beneath
her feet like tiny knuckles.
I sit at the window, drawing
her picture for the thousandth time
forgetting to shape her eyes
and her mouth, not knowing
where to shade the wrinkles
and sadness. She watches
from the doorframe
her hand holding her stomach
as if it contains something
and upstairs we both hear
the floorboards shift beneath
so many feet, each one a tongue
groaning a child's name
and then falling back into place
melting against the quiet.

Because Another Person Asked When We'd Start Having Children

We drink on the pack porch,
glow-in-the-dark balloons strung across the fence.
The beer is amber-rich and goes down quickly.
I've been smoking again, can smell it on your neck.
The dog barks at the window and we trace
each other's shadows, fumble, my hands in your back pocket.
Husband. What sweaty kisses we allow one another
in this heat. My lips swollen with them
and a sudden fever for you, your body.

Our friends make up drinking games
and we interrupt an otherwise quiet night,
your laugh too loud.
You persuade everyone to strip and jump
in a neighbor's pool. You've always been so persuasive.
The moon shining on the water pulls us
to one another, where we drift
as if we've always drifted
so calmly.

I wake early, nude, my body dry and sore,
your body turned away from me.
The echo of a dream lingers,
a baby's cries burning the walls.

Self Portrait with Aftermath

What I had thought would happen:
mostly, bonfires in the backyard,
hiking in the park, playing some
tennis in August heat, sitting
beneath a tree with books or with wine.

The heat settling over us.
Having sex on the staircase.
Our hands sweaty sails.

Instead, I am a distant
explosion of myself, remember
being a bomb. Your hands
over me collect steel fragments,
make shapes we have never
seen before, then destroy them.

You talk about my nipples
as if I'm in another room.

When I am cleaning the bathtub,
I think of Bruce Springsteen
fucking me from behind.
I chain smoke on the back porch
and flick my cigarettes
into pots where you have promised
to plant the flowers many times
and instead rain water fills them,
sours, and I use it to make
your morning coffee.

Thursday Autobiography: Astronomers Reveal Supernova Factory

In the morning, you pick magnolias and place them in water upside down. You want to see what drowning looks like. The hard petals resemble the shape of the day's bloom. I eat alone in the kitchen with a spoon. Glass spreads over the tile floor in pieces. I can see the shape of a wine glass there, a whiskey bottle there. A glass heart figurine there. I walk barefoot, wait for scent of blood. For sixty days, we create explosions in various rooms of the house. When you call, I want to know if you want your letters. If you have counted the cuts on your forearm. There must be blood in your car, trails of these supernovae glistening in footsteps. I wanted tulips, anyway. The shape of a closed flower. Something constant like dimples. You came. I didn't come. We both walk over the cloudy debris.

After Hours

When the bar closes, we walk to the old café
order soggy bacon, basted eggs.
We talk about how many hours
are in a grain of salt, how many
minutes we pepper across our plates.
My husband is at home
sleeping or watching porn
but we don't discuss him.
I know that later when I come home,
my husband will come, too, saying
baby, his eyes fully closed
and I will wonder what color
your breath is in the morning.
I will think violet, or the color
of echo, of impulse.
The café lights are tough,
demand that we look at one another
deeply, eyes squinting.
On the table, the glint
of syrup stains remind me
of your tongue. Often, I find
my husband's dimple
on your cheek and gag
pressing a fork to my mouth
a swollen harp, meditating
my husband away. It is January
or it is May. There may be snow
or a lightning storm. We will
watch from the window of the café
leaning, our hands crossing the table,
searching for crumbs.

Belated

When you are not dead
my dreams are in color.
You laugh into my sleep
with the blue melody of skin,
of sky. This is not a love
letter: Elegies are for ideas
as well as for lovers.

You have been an idea
waiting to be articulated
all these years.

You are an essay
on brown paper
written with matchsticks.

We say *fire*. We want
to say *failure*.

In one dream, you speak
from a podium in a blue
haze classroom. My hand
eternally raised toward you,
a severed wing.

Sometimes I wake to the song
of your name. A rock dove's
nocturnal whisper. Your breath
mimics a crow's.
When you leave, I find
feathers written into the sheets.

Restless Wonder

It's like this in the cold,
when the lover sends
each letter back, stamped red –

no person here by that name.
On a map our houses are so close
together, they might touch

or at least the vines
could eventually pass the border
and curl against both of us
at the same time.

Because I can't sleep
during the day, the garden
grows wild. Out of boredom,

I weed, to keep these dirty hands.
Another allergy attack
might push me forward in time

to a place where the body
breathes easily, where I can hang
onto a stream of light and balance
over a newly remodeled roof.

A hummingbird disguised as a bee
sends my body waving
across the lawn.

The light, *the light*
appears and I question
what they call silver lining

openings into distant hallways.
I'm reminded of the lover
touching a petal,

the flower disintegrating
into baking soda.
The smell of bleach, concrete.

The burying of last night's dream
and the others that came before.
Light bends at a chain link fence,
creating egg carton shadows

where I stitch blades of grass
over what remains
of a lover's face.

III

June's Child

Finally, I wanted to give up my grief,
the boiling cocoon wrapped in beeswax
and scent of burning lilac, the concrete
heaviness of my arms, the heat of cicadas

crossing my mother's bones, these dreams
entombed in chlorine and warm sheets.
My mother's quartz heart shined beneath
layers of dry dirt. I hadn't had it in me

to imagine something beyond the weather.
The thermometer on the back porch
had broken years before, or melted
from touch of tongue, hands checking.

Cemeteries bled dried grass, russet
and bronzed leaves, as if I kept dropping
flames the shape of my mother's eyes
or burned pearls. I didn't know callused

seasons kept returning. The char and burn
was natural, an element of my skin,
smelled of my mother's childhood home
catching fire, magnified petals, frying pan
spittle oil and grease, hot vapor.

Even in October, I'd find bath water
red as ulcers, or a child's jump rope
curled on a steely front porch like the recently
shed skin of a snake, crackling with steam.

Morning Comes

Paper snowflakes strewn across the living room carpet like so many egg shells. I rebuild the house around them, one wood panel at a time. Inside my body, a wind turbine, steel slicing clouds. Tumbleweeds scrape burs from my veins. Mother watches with her long wings, her fingers amnesiacs of gauze, blood. She spreads smoke with her lips, knits shapes like doors, unravels them. I won't remember the jasmine. Black wine burns over my lap, curling into my skirt and thighs. My fingers pull the flames over like waves. Sifting, I always come back to the steel cables in my limbs, to this rusty combine, tarnished December petals. I separate flames with my tongue. The house will wait. Father. Tarnish weeps in so many colors.

Why I Can't Return Your Call

When the mother dies,
the children don't know how to receive gifts.
Instead, they wait till the giver stops looking
to tear the paper slowly, in short strips,
practicing the many sounds of surprise
they've heard many times
from the throats of others.

Becoming Windows

She didn't want to die in a garage
on a Tuesday after watering geraniums,

after the sun burned the crab grass
into straw. Her arms were becoming

the things scarecrows dream of,
her joints replaced by gears and string.

There had been long nights on porches
and then suddenly the aftermath

of blackness. She didn't want
the cold star touch of morning.

She didn't want the army
of birds out back, fighting for nests.

She had once imagined curling
her body into a fist, and pressing

against the bricks for warmth.
Afternoons, coughing mufflers,

kept her inside. *Wait*. Wait.
She found a deep sadness

in the cleaning of wood floors
in the scent of a mowed lawn

in the way her body clicked
as if lacking sleep, how she cracked

like burning oak leaves.
She watched for the black birds

and waited for the snip of chain link
for dogs to barrel over her

drooling over her own lonely snarl.

Remains

After a bath, she opens an old bottle of Chardonnay, wiping dust across her cheek. Her skin red and warm. Her hands hold nothing. Each sip salt-weaved and tart, the wine kept so warm it cuts her gums. She coughs fizz and frowns. Taps a nail on the glass. Could she umbrella her loved ones, could she keep them from seeing what she has seen – vanilla rotting along shoulder blades, blown glass shattering in a child's palm, the way a river opens to drag farmland in. The dust has gotten so thick inside she can barely scrape it with a fingernail. Her hands shape globes of light. Lost trinkets follow some shallow current. She knows of retreat like this, the calm of forgetting. She begs the waters, follows the sound of a lover back indoors. A bedroom light is on somewhere, the call of burn that she knows all too well.

We Stop Writing About the Moon

We stop writing about Jupiter, about flying rings.

We stop listening to jazz, sew piano strings into our calves.

We bleed silver coins. Our bodies pretend to hear us. Our bodies are answers. We scoop mirrors onto our skin.

She said that a baby is not a woman's body. The baby does not attach itself, is not you. She said that the baby is its own body and knows it.

Blood lines the sheets.

He broke a plate by the river. An exploding flower.

We stop writing about petals, about fleshy blades.

She said god haters wore black and ate fog. The fog is the god hater's favorite breakfast. They make documentaries over these things. Watch them on TV channels where god haters are eaten in small forkfuls, where god haters are being fed to babies, one finger at a time.

Photosynthesis is ineffective on our wounds. We continue to mate in empty laundry rooms, in shower stalls, in elevators. Our bodies surprise us. Babies become babies when we show them how.

We have forgotten sky. How far we used to drive to get from one state to another.

Our fingers are our weapons. The only way to see ourselves is to do it in pieces.

She calls her friends on the phone. Tells them she found another one. They will turn this one. Fetuses line the walls in the grocery store, their decay a scent of bananas and powdered sugar. She will not see the fetuses no matter how many times she walks by them.

Consider the way a stapler works to hold things together. Imagine the ripping. Imagine the loss.

We stop holding hands like lovers. Sweat gets colder with age, slicker. Sometimes we laugh at the people on bicycles, but never know quite why. We erase our laughter. Replace it with curiosity. Replace it with bandages.

What We Have Forgotten

I rest on the sand with you
by the lake, its warmth receding

and we can't stay on the beach
because the water is a thousand tongues

waiting for us to get up and walk
into them with heavy pockets
while our burns knot in the mouths of fish.

We wait on our backs
for the earth to shift to a new position,

for planets to swarm away from us,
the dark womb sky revealing
what we have forgotten existed –

there are others out there with red knuckles
and scraped chins, but I am not saying

what I mean to say and you keep looking
toward the other side where a boat docks

and sways. Broken oars and cut ropes
resembling your hands
lie on someone's deck awaiting repair.

Autopsy of Me

Say you will pull at the seams of flesh that lie thin like floss or shadows along my body, as if between memory and action. Stretch blocks of skin revealing contours of black and sinew. Say the muscles look like rock canyons in Arizona, and you above, pointing, remember crawling through. Say my heart is the shape of a locust. Push your hand inside and reach to say I feel like a sponge. Say my blood is silky, the same substance as a cloud, that you are tempted to lick it. Say you will. Press an ear to a kidney. Listen for the softness, what you imagine, a bundle of postcards crumbled inside breathing, wet with me, blurred by my body. Say you find my hypochondria in a knot beneath my lung, wrapped and threaded. Cut the sutures. Let the black threads open, spidering inside me. Wipe the sickness over my lungs. Say it's the color of the ocean. Say it's the color of the ocean floor. Clean it. Anesthetize the corners of my mouth. Return my body to where you found it. Sewing, a cricket settles somewhere and sings, and there is always more.

After Moving

In my dreams, the house shapeshifts.
Rooms become staircases, doorways
become links to others' homes.
When I get lost, I wander into a party
and many people push me
to the center of living room.
Where is my husband? I ask,
and the faces steal windows,
wine glasses, all becomes dark.
I run from one room to the next.
Where is my husband? I crawl,
hide beneath beds, watch fathers
read stories to their children,
watch lovers rise from mattresses.
A bedroom becomes a bar.
A woman sits at the corner
and I know I am to ask her –
the one with the pearls on,
the one drinking gin and tonics.
She whispers the name of our
building, and I write it down.
Where is my husband? The question
becomes less of a search
for a body, and more of an urge.
This looking, this unknowing,
the house that changes shape
and shuts windows right before me.
When they begin chasing me,
I drop a glass of wine
only to watch it suspend
spill nothing, only to trip

over a laundry basket.
There will be ledges, somehow
I know. There will be
waiting in the sky.
Where is my husband
will become *where are my hands.*
If I do find him, he will act
as though I'd been there all along.
He will act as though
we'd never separated
to begin with.
Where is my husband
will become
where have you been.

Poem for Fire

This poem was written in the dark
with wet matches lining the window sill,

gasoline on my fingertips, candles
burning in the closet where wax spread

lonely, unbound like my mouth.
I wait to mold words, to conjure

the empty vowels of your name
as if creating a limb, a face.

Isn't this what fire does? Create,
in long scraping arcs, necrosis

of wood and drywall. Black
edges and burned faces,

noses of splinter, charcoal
silhouettes, disintegration.

As humans we find faces
in everything, a natural urge

for us to connect to the light
in another's eyes or the secrets

in another's lips. We are searchers
of sparks. A single dimple

ignites reaction: how long
can we look into something

before we find meaning transported
from our own blackening

photographs and curled edges,
our own crumbling reflections.

The Emptiness Begins

In the morning, when I wake
and realize the pregnancy only a dream.
I rub my palms over my stomach
until I am sure nothing stirs inside.

When I find that I can reach
through to the wings of my lungs,
there is calm.

The days are blotted
with slick seeds.
Babies with large, egg-shaped heads
turn to watch my empty arms.

At the grocery store
I buy more eggs
and learn to eat them
one by one in the dark.

The Widower

At his doorstep, you find phantoms,
blooms distorting the soil.
Bent and crushed stems
leaking pulp to wood panels.
Each ghost on the porch
lilac or twisting orchid.
When you knock, stale lace
and fingernail dust shakes from the house.
He tattoos a single bee on his arm
for each year they are apart,
so when he finally reaches for you
you look for nests along the curve
of his chest, the threat of swarm.
You know the scent of honeysuckle
on his pillow, lining the walls.
The house you move around
is shaped like her body, is dressed
in the silks and skirts she wore for him.
The floorboards only collapse at night
while he breathes on his aged brass bed.
Even then, splinters curl up to you,
the scrape of her ruby and glass, antique,
across your skin. After dinner, you wash
your hands in the master bathroom, know
this old soap will linger long after you leave
the room, and still, he walks over your body.
His arms, their faded yellow and black knots,
pass over the curves of your breast, find her
nestled where he opens you and looks inside.
Nights like this, when you are both looking,
the curtains wave against the windows, the whirl of her hips.

Sister

Black light dust in your palm
tastes of burn.

Cut up Barbie doll legs
sit on your book shelf.

Once, we brushed each other's hair
so long static entered our fingers.

Each time we touch
palm to metal,
the sharp slice
of want, of doll
face.

This mirror clicks
into place behind us.
Our backs take notice,
turn and twist, spines
crackling like Barbie's limbs.

Toss that lipstick tissue
out of the window.

You waltz into my dreams
with long fingernails
and gothic lipstick.
Your mouth curves out
in stitches. How many times
have you re-woven the threads?

The moon enters your back room.
You sit at your desk, hunched,
the knuckles of your spine
bleeding wine.

It is here we once cried
over dead mothers.
It is here we found our faces
on one another's palms.

Barbie's head in the trash can.
She smiles
among broken beer bottles.

Once, we looked for fathers
in the cool concrete outside
in stale coffee on the counter.

Have you looked beneath the bed
for paper cuts?

Each time we build
a house around ourselves
we leave out windows.

We walk in and out of rooms.

Pull the dangling threads
from my elbows and lips.

Preface to a Late Night Text

In the morning, I'll have deleted it already:
the winter, your thumbs, the sound
of your sigh over a beer glass.
Once, I swore I'd marry you
after the snow, but the leaves
had already frozen to the porch
building a nest of frost, tongue, silt.
If you'd accepted me
when I'd asked,
we'd be scattered, singed postcards,
half-written notes.
We'd hold winter in our palms
like a shard of light.
If you'd accepted me
when I'd asked –
we'd be scattered, singed postcards,
half-written notes.
We'd hold winter in our palms
like a shard of light.
the startle of a perfumed flashback
your arms draped over a balcony
the threat of *jump* and leaves
on my windshield in the morning.
When you wake, it will be as if
you'd never chosen
the Wolverine beard or the cashier
from the corner gas station
and I'll blow smoke into the air,
walking right on through it.

At Dawn

All the flames have dimmed,
each window nothing more than a quiet space

nestled in the dark, and each gold sigh
nodding toward the sun. I wait

for the moan of bodies to move
about the house, as if I've slept
more than a few hours since you've gone –

What sounds a body makes
as it tries to fall asleep, the shock

of bone gravity. I press into the bed
waiting, the rock you promised I would become.

I want the windows to guide you home,
to pull you back from the shadows

and sludge, to bring you
to me whole, ghost-faced and whispering.

Wrap me in your tobacco breath
once more. Face me on this bed.

Feel it bend beneath both our bodies.
In the other room, a cradle rocking
side to side groans our mothers' bones.

Bone Cartography

What kind of map is this, hung upside down on your back, un-ironed lines only visible in certain light? What cities our torsos contain and hide away in the retreating moments of breath, sighing *lights out lights out lights out* until we turn back. North and south do not exist. Your hands cast shadows on a far-reaching wall and behind you, paper wings stretch like roads twisting in a surrealist painting. This is how I know we've gone off course. When I look at a road it is simply a road, and when I hear your feet on gravel, I sense the making of bones, a compass cracking in the cold, a wintery laugh. Remain open to the cravings direction will provide you, but do not hold your breath.

IV

Quit Day

Let's say you wake, every ashtray
tossed into the garbage can the night

before and you can nearly smell the rust
smearing your arms as you imagine dragging

each one out to hide in your home.
Let's say you pace the rooms, toss

the smoke-stained mattress in the front yard,
bring the hose inside and wet the walls.

You will keep moving. You will rid the home
of the scent you've opened every morning

for ten years. Let's say you plant palm trees
in the basement, wipe the baseboards

with cooking grease. Put a cake in the oven
and eat nearly all of it in one day, by hand.

The kitchen is a panic room, all carrots
and pumpkin pie and memories of standing.

Let's say you invite your friends over
and they flick their butts into the garden

and clouds groan out of the ground.
They watch you wrap cinnamon sticks

in wax paper, light each end, place the burn
to your lips, fingertips, nipples. You have been

half-naked all along, ironing palm leaves, mopping
with whiskey. Let's say you calm one day,

sit at a table with a glass of red wine. A lover stands
at the other end of the room smoking a Marlboro,

full flavor, offers you his hand. Let's say you
give in to one last cigarette and the trees turn

greener, the sky opens till it's perfectly flat.
The day becomes brighter till it's not.

Let's say you watch the lover leave
and the charcoal footprints and the bruises

lift from your sleepy lungs,
your panty line visible behind all the smoke.

Love Letter for Virtual Particles

We were there on a Wednesday, holding onto buoys of broken light. Within a vacuum, we are able to disappear and reappear, moving in and out of existence. To reach out is to capture photons in our palms, smooth them over like small stones, to watch them light up in our fingers. Once, we found blue electrons like scraps at the foot of the bed. Light fits in the creases of envelopes and there are more love letters where this one came from. How little energy is needed or expended. Words like neon lights within the wrinkles by our eyes. Bodies make noises beneath covers like harps. Blueing down. Sometimes I think we are water, blurred currents. Here. I will latch myself to the space between light and your blue. As if I can exist when I decide to. As if pressed between palms. As if swallowing light enough times will make my tongue into some kind of tropical bird.

The Widow

Black lace panties scattered
across hardwood floors –
she walks over them, skids
barefoot when she wakes

to empty vases crumbling
in dark cabinets. Someone
sprays perfume in the hall
every twenty minutes, exhales

and sprays again. Musk,
this scent of ginger shampoo
suddenly a man's leather belt.
She wakes remembering sex

with another woman, climbs
onto her bed again to re-dream him
into the day. When he rises
he is smoke, is mist. Empties

into the sky. Her ring finger
burns, this halo stitching
made of acid, of flame.

What wonders the walls speak
when she curls against them,
each vertebrae snapping off
like tiny planets dusting the night.

She thinks of his mahogany
casket. Slices raspberries
on a white plate. Tucks
her shirt in, hides the curves

of her breasts. She touches
picture frames each night,
smears greased palms over glass
right across his glossed face.

What a Lover Asks

Bring me the whisper balm
and I'll spread it
over your aching knee.
Where we find
the tender, we experience
splinter. Nightly, your anxious
palms cradle a down-filled
space. This *is*.
Bring me what grows
between you and your arms.
Bring me the hourglass sonnet,
the hamster wheel, the video camera,
the horses. This home wants
buried beneath tie-dyed tongues.
Struggle. Bring me my body
to dance in a dark mouth.
Bring me burned psalms
the remains of a graveyard brawl.
In bed, your fingertips confetti
our sighs,
burst open the want
of a pearl.

On Our Last Visit

The water was inside us, ruffling
our lungs and intestines. It drew lines
on our tendons, marked us
for muscle erosion, for drowning.

The skylight in the guest room
dropped rain water to our bed,
until a pulsing ravine ruined
the sheets – I found you knotted,
wrecked in wet blankets each morning.

The sound of sea shells crumbling
reminds me of your laughter
that summer, its hollow crack,
the way a smile might move

through me, your breath weighted
with the suspense of a water balloon.
I always worried it would break
over me, cold and blue,
your wreckage scattering.

Uptight Flamingos Will Only Have Sex to Marvin Gaye Slow Jams

Later, in the bedroom, you'll undress me
or I'll undress in front of you, and we'll
stop mid-way because something you mutter
makes me uncomfortable, like that time you
said *Tell me you like this, this* before I even
let you inside me, and the way my limbs
became empty corn stalks and I tugged
my underwear back on because I had to
start over, and you'll always keep saying
how sorry you are, it's about the moment,
you get so into it, you just want me so bad
and I'll really know that if I don't close
my own eyes, I'll watch you too closely,
find a new gray hair in your mustache
or count ceiling fan blades or imagine
us in the same bed at sixty. We'll always
have to start over, try a re-do,
make it work somehow, even on laundry day
or in your mother's home or in the car
while I think of grain bins or medical bills
or your brother's new job or what we'll
have for dinner each night that coming week,
when we've promised to do it at least
twice a week because all the studies say
that couples who make love more
are truly happier. I'll ask you to change
the music, and change it again, or turn
it down, and you won't hear me
and my hands will move too quickly
to catch up to your hands, and I'll apologize

for all your apologies, so much breath,
and when it finally happens, and we remember
how to move or where to place our hands,
it won't be that awful, and we'll forget
how long it took to get there,
how tricky it is to allow the body to open,
to let all that sunlight in.

Portrait of a Girl Drawn with Neophobia

If she braided sidewalks. If she spit egg shells,
ran, knife-ready, arms cradling nests. Remembered
being kerosene, asking trees for a light. What wind
looks like from above. The sound of *amen* smoke-heavy.
Her nipples pressing against a soft shirt. If incense
burns her thighs. If her hands were not shaped like leaves.
An impossible December builds hives around her feet.
She trundles, cuts the skirt from the bed. Takes gasoline
with her meds. If she sings ghost pepper. The night tying
a draw string around her home, the black milk-chrome
breath of a lover in the act of confession. She breathes.
If she mapped it again. If she bent over the sink, took him
to the waters. If she cried out and cried out. If she shuddered
feathers. Legs bleeding the whole drive home.

The Meaning of More

We stack glass jars in the hallway
and fill them with fireflies and nails.
From the bed, we discover
walls move like water,
the blanket a psychic's tongue
draped across our legs.
What is *more* but what we can't
really touch, your body sliding
down the shower wall,
where you end up when you
are gone. Spaces left
unstirred down my back.
Bury me in your mattress
and dig me out later in loose threads,
unstitching notes,
the cigarette-glow
of need. We are objects
like the things we keep
stored in boxes and attics,
these lonely trinkets, bed sheets.
Keep the pillows from long ago
your lovers' names sketched
inside each one, languages
of dead petals, wild pearls.
This bed shifts continuously,
a palm cupping us
over a waiting pool
where everything rises.

Your Name is a Shape Made in the Mouths of Magicians

After you die, magicians line the sidewalk in long metallic robes. They perform with fractured concrete smiles, stitches hanging from the corners, hold fly wings in their palms until their hands glisten. The newspapers do not speak of your death or of anyone else's. Tonight the moon will hang as if it's a paper clip in the sky, sleek and silver and bendable. Won't you hang from it, or fold pieces of sky like paper into origami flowers. Once, you folded a swan and it flew away in white pieces. Flutter, flutter. The magicians speak your name as a spell. We meditate on the lawn waiting for the color of water, for your abstract silhouette to fold and re-fold over us, unshadowing. When we drop your casket into the river, it shifts north, becomes a paper boat.

Poem for Apology

I woke up to write about apology
from the view of a dreamer
with fish tails and black water
and front yard wrecks, tornado debris.
Yet, here, the dreamer is more
like a planner: *We will do this, yes,*
it will happen.
Dreamers accomplish, finish,
rather than flail along some broken plane
of light, bleeding and lonely.
In my home, apology is shaped
like a fork, most days, its points
nudging skin, twisting.
The dreamer finds the scent
of apology cucumber-melon, leather.
Apology is bathing together,
washing each other's backs
with a loofa, holding on
with only suds between you.
Even the dreamers can't plan
for this – for the fingers
lit like sparklers crackling over skin,
the prick and snap of desire.
We wait to find traces
later in the dark
when the memory of apology
lights onto our skin
and dissipates into neon, then black,
blinking into the mattress.

Reaches And

    This month brings cardboard boxes
to our porch like coffins
you fill with books, towels,
pills, crying, and maps –

    the things you take with you
every June when you decide
it's time to go. This place
haunts with smolder and sweat,

    you say. It's too hard
to walk in the sun and not think
about it, the wind bleeding
clouds onto your fingers,

    the low growl of thunder
burning against your back,
the ocean we can't reach.

    When you are gone, I reach
across the quilt to touch you,
but find only sand-grit, June's
breath, gravel dust

    burning under my fingertips.
Everything is an ocean to you,
even when it's dry sand
flung in our eyes,

    even when it's November
and we sit under trees in a park
in Kansas, the browned grass a font
of ocean you have yet to learn.

    Still, I know what comes
after June, that you will fill
this room again. Your boxes
will empty, saltwater staining your things,

    the scent of oysters in your hair,
your skin as alabaster, as crisp
and easy to crumble as shell.

    Soon, we'll eat sushi on the patio
at your favorite restaurant and
reach for the ocean with our tongues,
our feet touching beneath the table.

Our Home Becomes an Island

You grill lobster early, dragging shrimp from the sea. Large nets lasso our front porch.

The beach shifts overnight. Dream seaweed, birds returning.

Water reminds me of breaking. On the new shore, water turns from blue to charcoal. People jump off roofs into the wet. Piles of clothes float like clumps of seaweed. We hear many children screaming.

We have been to Carolina. Want it braided into us. Want the edges and sand-burned shores to collapse our home. You reminisce. Smudged hands. Dry paper.

Water smells of tornadoes, of land-locked yachts.

We write odes to past lovers. You burn the paper, toss it into the water, like so much searching, like so many voices dropping into a bowl. The emptying of a home is a baptism we keep reliving. We eat tuna. Walk on the backs of whales.

If only, Carolina. Instead, I empty ghosts from my wound. Bury rosaries in sand.

We build sails on the roof. Waves fling pearls against our windows. Click, click.

Another child is born in North Carolina. Its jellyfish limbs poison its mother's skin. Wet burns. Barnacles raking fist-shaped lungs.

Final Quiet

Because I can't say the word
cunt, my lover teases me.
In the bedroom, I talk
mattress, I talk tiger lilies
watch his lips mangle
against my belly button.
There are many words
he thinks I should say:
Cock, cum, love.
I roll over, unable
to rid myself of the image
of penis-shaped ladders
vining down a dark well.
In his apology, I smell
a coalmine, think of sliding.
It's not that I'm embarrassed,
but that the words
sit like rocks in my mouth,
fill my cheeks, mean almost
nothing. I remember saying
the word *yo-yo* as a child,
over and over so many times
it became *yellow*
until the sun split in tow
and dropped over me
while I slept. In this room
the lover weaves whiskey
into quilts until all the words
I've ever known
discover a final quiet
bury an echo in my thigh

a turning windmill
a thread untangling

The Ways We Wake

In the afternoon, frost-hemmed, the curtains
remain. Your liquor cabinet smile moves
across living rooms, porches, thighs.
    You won't discuss
the ways we wake, how it tastes to bite down
on dream. My body wants to find
windows and handprints, winged imprints
on the pillow-top mattress. A hand
can press only so far, like we can only
wake so many times before we know
how to count wallpaper flowers
with one long look.
We learn which rooms to choose
to finish dreams. You erase tile patterns
with your tongue, watch me straighten
myself across another floor
like a lonely antenna.
You are cold antiseptic polishing
doorknobs and taste buds. A vinegar
wash upon waking sunburned and feverish.
Today reminds you of yesterday
but I am busy building tomorrow
on the seat of a lawn mower,
waiting for the hum of a lover.
We find sand and snow in the same
envelopes, burn bills in the basement,
make sculptures with shot glasses,
draw lines on each other's backs
with our fingers.

Digging for Wasps

I've never said this to a stranger before: it's best to ignore sounds in a neighbor's backyard, the rusted swing sets, ghosts on another's doorstep. Houses smile from the front sidewalk. Work your way back and find gutters fallen, so many dead limbs bent across a lawn, like reaching arms. At night, a hum releases from cracked foundations, and in basements, black mold spreads its spackled tongue. Keep walking when you find children under porches feeding on wasp nests, fathers with guns, mothers sewing fences within fences. No matter how hard you stop and look, how much water you find in the lungs of a newborn, there is only the nest. There is only so much sifting. Only twigs and sand.

Acknowledgements

Poems from *One Last Cigarette* have previously appeared in the following publications.

- "Quit Day," "Poem for Apology," and "Portrait of a Couple with an Overdrawn Checking Account" in *Stirring*

- "Pisces Elegy," "Arsonist," and "Reaches And-" in the chapbook *Aching Buttons*, by Dancing Girl Press. "Pisces Elegy" was first published by *Blood Lotus*.

- "Evening Litany" in *Meat for Tea*

- "Alone, Before His Birth," and "The Widow" in *I-70 Review*

- "When the Bourbon Settles" in *The River Journal*

- "Before the Diagnosis" (published under the title "Before you Die") and "We Stop Writing About the Moon" in *Phantom Limb*

- "Winter Myths" and "Our Home Becomes an Island" in *Menacing Hedge*

- "Overflow" in *San Pedro River Review*

- "He Drew Me From Behind" in *North Central Review*

- "Where to Place Hands" in *A-Minor*

- "A Night Without Stars" in *Flutter Poetry Journal*

- "Self-Portrait with Aftermath" in *Eclectic Eel*

- "Thursday Autobiography" in *Lingerpost*

- "Belated" in *Atticus Review*

- "June's Child" in *Thrush Poetry Journal*

- "Becoming Windows" and "After Moving" in *Rose and Thorn Journal*

- "Autopsy of Me" in *Mid-American Review*

- "The Widower" in *Midwestern Gothic*

- "Sister" in *Connotation Press*

- "Love Letter for Virtual Particles" in *Jelly Bucket*

- "Portrait of a Girl Drawn with Neophobia" in *Mixed Fruit*

- "The Meaning of More" in *The Bookends Review*

- "Digging for Wasps" in *Santa Fe Lit Review*

- "Researchers Discover Insomniac Birds are the Sexiest Birds" in *Dressing Room Journal*

- "Woman Discovers Creepy Ex Boyfriend Living in Attic," "Bury," and "What a Lover Asks" in *Poetic PinUp Review*

Also by Honest Publishing

Wedding Underwear for Mermaids
Linda Ann Strang

The Killing of a Bank Manager
Paul Kavanagh

Nothing Doing
Willie Smith

Jazz
Jéanpaul Ferro

The Wooden Tongue Speaks
Bogdan Tiganov

The Vorrh
B. Catling

Iceberg
Paul Kavanagh

Homegirl!
Ryder Collins

www.ingramcontent.com/pod-product-compliance
Lightning Source LLC
LaVergne TN
LVHW041632070426
835507LV00008B/578